WITHDRAWN

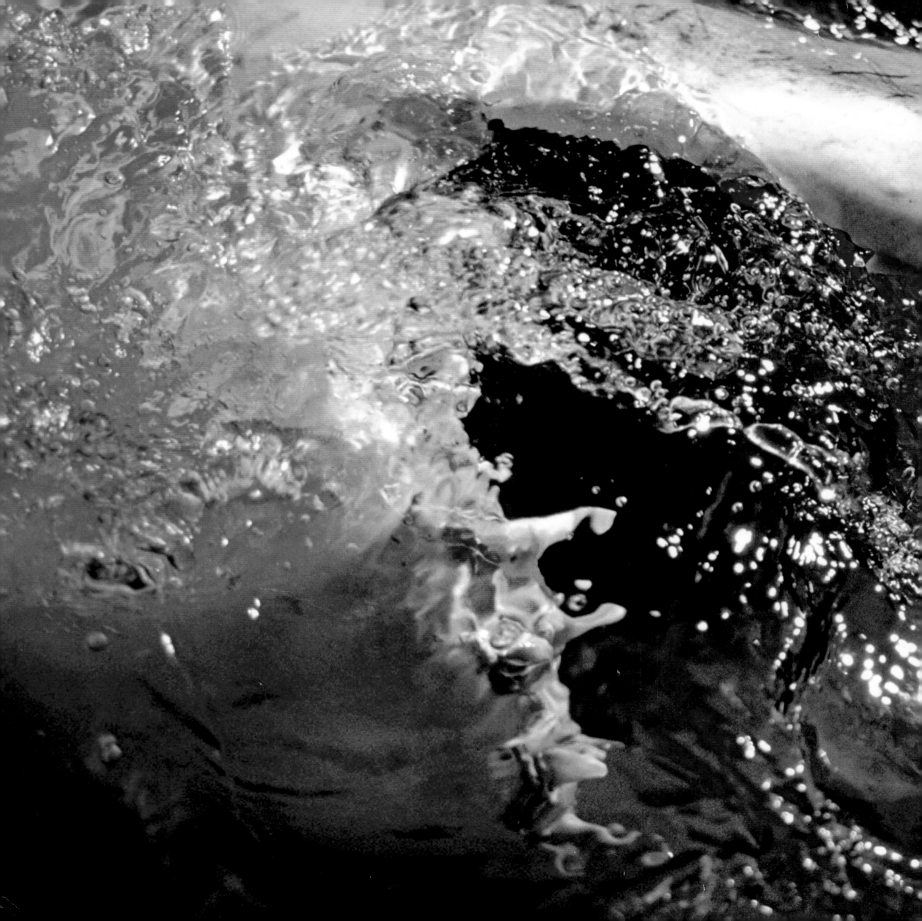

FACE TO FACE WITH
SHARKS

by David Doubilet and Jennifer Hayes

NATIONAL
GEOGRAPHIC
WASHINGTON, D.C.

David with his camera after photographing great white sharks. Shark cages have metal bars that are wide enough for cameras to fit in but close enough to protect us.

FACE TO FACE

A 16-foot-long great white shark bites our steel shark cage near Dangerous Reef, South Australia. A white shark can open its mouth wide enough to swallow a whole seal or a human.

We like sharks. My partner and co-author David and I spend many days a year in the water. We photograph all kinds of sea life and shipwrecks, but sharks are our favorite subject. David saw his first shark when he was 13 years old. The sandbar shark was bigger than he was! He was scared, but he still took a picture of it. I saw my first shark when a fisherman caught a big hammerhead nearby. When he cut it open, 20 perfectly formed baby sharks were inside of her. I was sad that the pups would not

HOW NOT TO GET EATEN BY A SHARK

Very few people are attacked by sharks each year. But sometimes sharks do attack, so here are some tips on how not to get eaten by one:

— Do not swim where people are fishing or dumping bloody fish guts into the sea. Sharks may mistake you for a fish.

— If you cut yourself and you are bleeding, get out of the water.

— Do not swim at dawn or dusk.

— Always swim with other people nearby.

— Never touch a shark!

survive. Right then, I knew I wanted to learn more about sharks and decided that one day I would go to school to study them.

We have photographed hundreds of sharks around the world. Different shark species have different personalities. Sand tiger sharks are calm, and we can swim with them. Great white sharks are very fast, aggressive predators, so we photograph them from a special shark cage. We are always excited to see a shark while we are diving, but we are always careful and cautious because we are visitors in their world.

We have never been bitten by a shark. However, some sharks try to bite our camera strobe lights. The sharks sense the batteries' electric charge, and they think the strobes are alive and might taste good.

You never know when you will discover a shark surprise. One day we were swimming in eight-foot-deep water off the coast of Tasmania, a large island south of Australia. We looked down and saw more than 15 sawsharks with long snouts, called rostrums, hiding in green algae. We were shocked to see them there because sawsharks usually live in over 100 feet of water. These female sharks may have come into shallow water to birth their pups.

We had our favorite shark dive on a very calm day off Gansbaai, South Africa. We got in our round metal cage and went in. Right away, a 15-foot great white swam out of the gloom and smashed our cage hard enough to knock us down. She came back to the cage again and again, showing us her razor-sharp teeth and a mouth that could swallow us whole. More and more great whites appeared out of nowhere. Four sharks circled our cage at the same time. We stayed in the cage until the sun went down, even though we were cold. That day, 17 different great white sharks came to check us out. It was the best day ever!

Shark expert Mark Addison named this tiger shark Barbara Ann. She and many other tiger sharks migrate to Aliwal Shoal off South Africa every year. Tiger sharks have beautiful stripes, but like tigers, they can be aggressive and unpredictable.

Sand tiger sharks are called ragged tooth sharks in Africa because of their scary teeth.

MEET THE SHARK

A 2,000-pound white shark leaps out of the water while chasing a cape fur seal in False Bay, South Africa. This behavior is called a breach.

Sharks are fish without bones. Their skeletons are made of flexible cartilage, like our noses and ears. They are good hunters, twisting and turning like underwater jet fighters. Sharks have been on Earth for 400 million years, surviving mass extinctions, ice ages, and hungry dinosaurs.

It is easy to spot a male shark. Males have two long, tube-like organs, called claspers, that hang under their bodies. Males use the claspers to fertilize the female's eggs.

➡ *Horn sharks lay corkscrew-shaped egg cases. This horn shark embryo was taken from its egg, but it is still attached to a sac of yolk that would have fed it as it grew inside the egg.*

➡ *Adult horn sharks have pig-like snouts and flat teeth that grind up urchins and shellfish. Sharp spines next to their dorsal fins protect them from predators. Females lay a pair of eggs every 11 to 14 days for about four months. They can lay up to 24 eggs in one season!*

Some sharks lay eggs in the sea, but most give birth to a litter of live babies, called pups. Pregnancy can last from eight months to two years. Most sharks have litters of 10 to 40 pups, but the sand tiger shark has only 2 pups. The blue shark can have over 135 pups at a time, but few survive.

Sharks can smell blood and feel the vibrations

of a struggling fish hundreds of yards away. They also have a secret weapon called electroreception. They feel the faint electrical field that surrounds all living things. If we could blindfold a hammerhead shark, it could still find a stingray buried in the sand by sensing the ray's weak electrical signal.

Most sharks have good eyesight. They are very sensitive to light, and they can see better in the dark than we do. Great white sharks have poked their heads out of the water and looked right at us in our boat. They can see above and below water, just like we can. Some sharks even have a special eyelid called the nictitating membrane that slides

This lemon shark has just given birth in the warm shallow waters of the Bahamas. The pup is still attached to the mother by a placental cord. The cord will stretch and break, and the pup will swim into nearby mangroves for protection from other predators.

A scientist examines the tiny razor teeth of a cookie cutter shark caught 3,000 feet below the surface in Suruga Bay, Japan. At right, this dolphin fish in the Bahamas has a perfectly round bite from a cookie cutter shark.

across the eye to protect it when they attack prey.

Sharks can't chew, but they still eat everything in the sea, from shrimp to small whales. They bite, shake their heads, and tear away chunks of flesh. Biting is hard business, and their teeth fall out all the time. But you will never see a toothless shark, because they never run out of teeth. They have rows of new teeth ready to take their place.

Different kinds of sharks have different kinds of

← *A great white shark attacked this cape fur seal in False Bay, South Africa. The wounded seal swam into shallow water and died.*

SKIN OF THEIR TEETH

Shark skin is a collection of tiny "skin teeth" known as dermal denticles. Each denticle has a tiny spike that points backward toward the tail. The denticles create a slip stream around the shark that lets it swim quickly and quietly.

— Going for the gold: Some swimmers wear swimsuits that are designed like shark skin. The suits help reduce drag, increase speed, and win medals.

— Like teeth, a shark's denticles are constantly lost and replaced throughout its life.

teeth. Some have flat plates for crushing food. Others have curved teeth for holding slippery fish or pointed, razor-sharp teeth for slicing and tearing. A deepwater shark called the cookie cutter has the oddest bite of all. This little 20-inch-long (50 cm) shark uses its thick lips to attach itself like a suction cup to a large fish, whale, or dolphin. It spins itself around, using a row of saw-like teeth to cut out a round "cookie" of flesh.

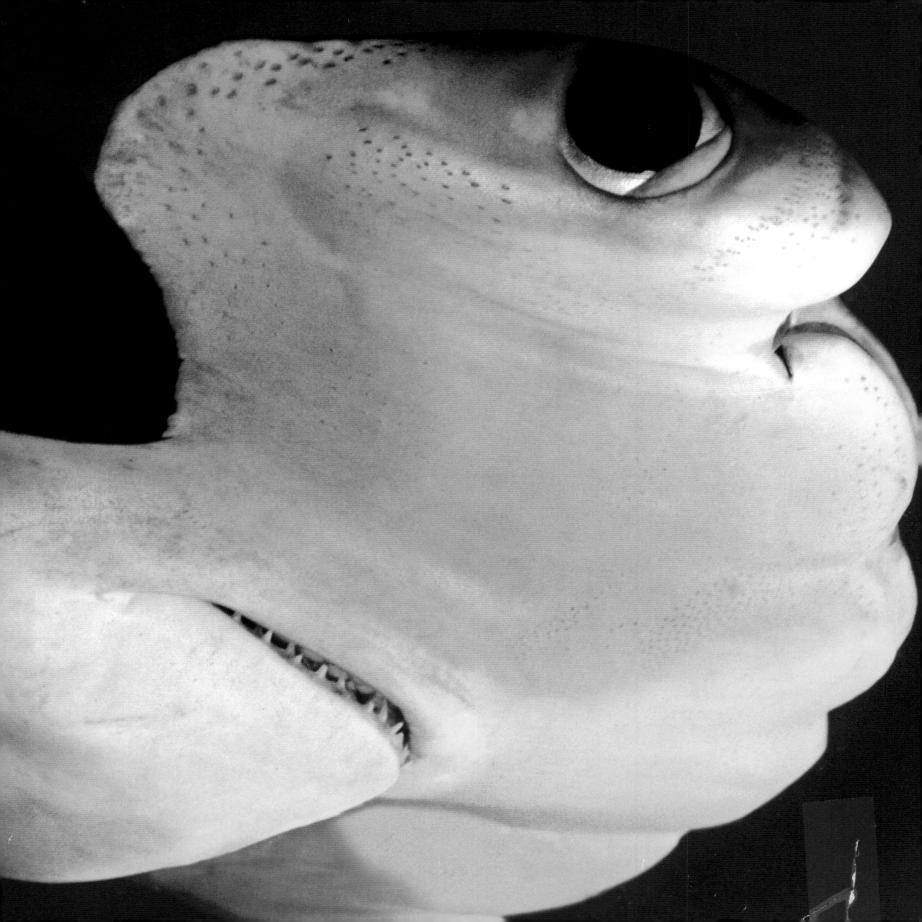

A Caribbean reef shark rests on the bottom of a cave. Many sharks must keep swimming in order to breathe, but some can lie still for long periods of time.

WORLD OF SHARKS

This 10-foot scalloped hammerhead shark was caught on a longline and set free. Their unusual heads and special vertebrae help them turn sharply. They often form large schools of over 100 sharks that swim together.

Sharks live everywhere in the ocean. They live in the frozen Arctic and in warm tropical lagoons. They live in the deep sea and in ankle-deep water. Some sharks, like the bull shark, can live in freshwater. In scary movies, sharks are sleek killing machines, but real sharks come in all sorts of wild and crazy shapes and sizes. They can be guitar shaped, cigar shaped, or flat as a pancake. They can be prickly or silky smooth, hammer-headed or pig faced, the size of your hand or as big as a bus.

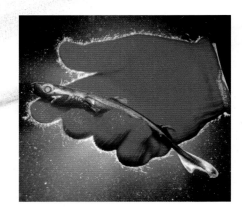

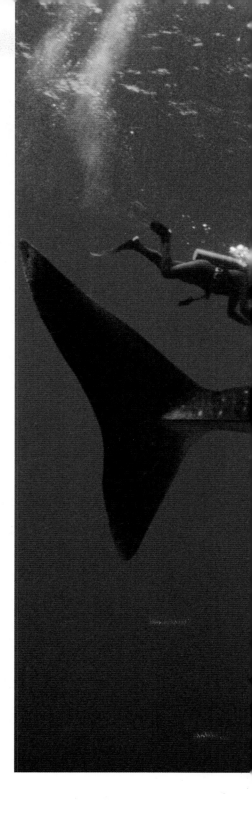

➡️ *A scientist holds a dwarf lantern shark, one of the smallest sharks in the world. Whale sharks are the world's largest sharks. The 40-foot-long whale shark at right was part of a large gathering off Ningaloo Reef in Australia.*

Experts who study sharks and other fish are called ichthyologists. They have described about 400 species of sharks, but the ocean is a big place, and new ones are still being found. One exciting recent shark discovery is megamouth, a secretive 15-foot (5-meter) deepwater shark that takes in seawater and strains food from it. Scientists have also found a two-foot-long (60-cm) catshark that uses its fins to walk across the seafloor. They call it the "walking shark."

The smallest sharks in the world live in the deepest parts of the sea. Cigar-sized sharks, like the dwarf lantern and pygmy shark, feed on shrimp and squid nearly a mile down. The whale shark is the biggest shark in the world. It can be more than 40 feet (12 meters) long. The second-largest shark, the basking shark, grows to over 30 feet (9 meters) long. These

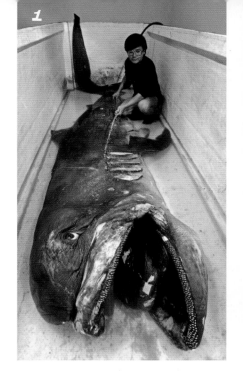

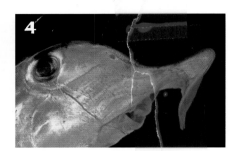

There are over 400 shark species in all sizes and shapes. 1. Megamouth is a deepwater filter feeder. 2. Oceanic white tip sharks are open-water predators. 3. The foot-long puffadder shark curls up like a cat. 4. Elephant sharks dig in the soft sea bottom with their trunk-like snouts. 5. The epaulette, or "walking shark," uses its pectoral fins like feet to walk across the seafloor. 6. A wobbegong shark awaits prey in an old oil drum. 7. Sawsharks use their long snouts to search for prey.

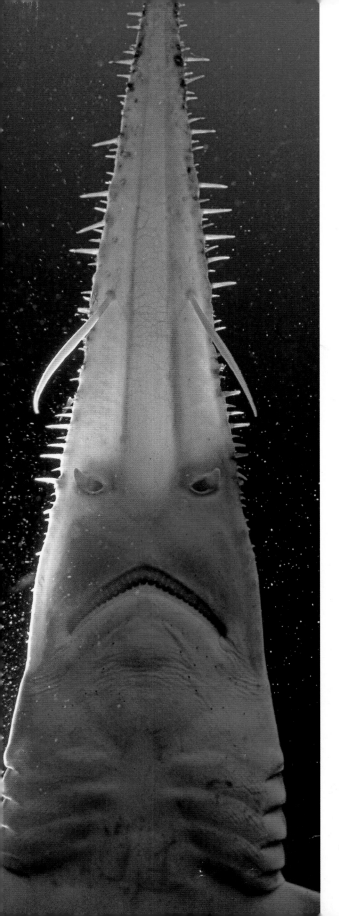

harmless, slow-moving filter feeders open their huge mouths and strain thousands of tons of water an hour to get to the tiny organisms called plankton.

The great white shark is one of the world's scariest predators. They mainly eat large fish, rays, and marine mammals like seals, sea lions, and dolphins. A few have attacked surfers. Still, they are not the fastest sharks—that's the mako shark, which can swim up to 30 miles per hour (48 kph) and can leap 20 feet (7 meters) in the air. The oceanic white tip shark is another fierce predator that lives offshore. Closer to shore, tiger and bull sharks patrol the shallow waters. They eat everything from sea turtles to birds. Sometimes, they attack humans.

Not all sharks hunt big prey. The puffadder shyshark curls up like a cat when it's threatened. Horn sharks, sometimes called pig sharks, have no sharp teeth. They use hard plates in their mouths to crush shellfish. The sawshark uses its long rostrum to sweep through the soft sea bottom looking for prey. The wobbegong shark is a slow-moving carpet shark that looks like a bath mat. But watch out! They may look like they're sleeping when they're not. They're quick, and their curved teeth don't let go.

This fistful of fins in a Tokyo fish market will end up as an expensive bowl of shark fin soup. Millions of sharks a year are killed just for their fins.

CONSERVATION

A large school of Caribbean reef sharks gathers under our dive boat in Nassau, Bahamas. The Bahamas is one of the few places in the world that still has a healthy population of sharks.

Every year David and I see fewer sharks in the sea. We have spent the last five years diving on coral reefs in Indonesia, and we have not seen any large sharks. Many sharks and big fish such as grouper have disappeared from reefs all over the world. Where have all the sharks gone?

Humans kill more than 100 million sharks every year. Most sharks are caught and killed on purpose for sport or food. Fishermen catch them on long-lines (long commercial fishing lines with hundreds

➡️ *A row of dead porbeagle sharks for sale at a Tokyo fish market. Porbeagle sharks are listed as "vulnerable to extinction" because they live a long time, mature late, and have only four pups a year.*

CAN YOU SEE ME NOW?

Sharks are masters of disguise! Sometimes they seem to disappear right in front of us. This helps them sneak up on their prey.

— How do you hide the biggest fish in the world? Giant whale sharks are covered in bright white dots. The spots make them almost invisible in bright sunlight.

— Wobbegong sharks look like they are wearing a mask. They have fleshy fringe beards around their mouths that look and move just like waving seaweed.

of hooks) and in fishing nets. Sometimes the sharks are caught in nets set to catch other fish. This accidental catch is called bycatch.

Most countries do not regulate shark fishing. We have even seen unborn shark pups and 100-year-old whale sharks on Asian menus. Whale sharks are sometimes called tofu sharks because of their soft white flesh. Shark cartilage and liver oil are used for medicine and cosmetics.

Most sharks are killed for a bowl of soup. Shark fin soup is an expensive Chinese delicacy. Fishermen catch sharks, cut off their fins, and throw the

↑ Shark expert Stuart Cove carefully feeds Caribbean reef sharks in the Bahamas. Thousands of people a year come here to dive and to learn about sharks.

sharks back into the sea, dead or alive. This is called shark finning. Without their fins, the sharks can't swim. They slowly sink to the bottom, where they can suffer for a long time before they suffocate or are eaten by other animals. Some countries have stopped shark finning, but shark fins are valuable. One pound of shark fin can sell for $300, and sets

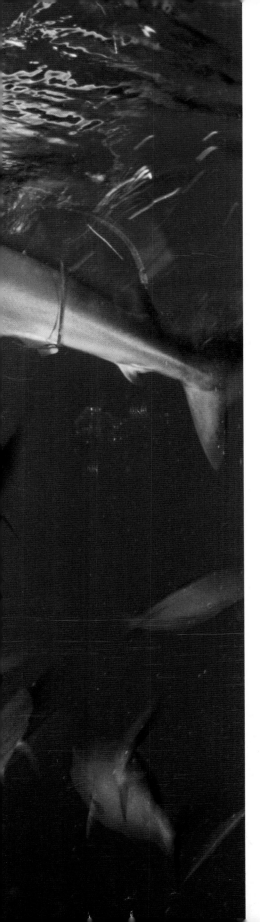

← *Cuba's Caribbean reefs are a rare example of an unfished and healthy coral reef system. Healthy populations of sharks contribute to a stable reef in these waters. Silky sharks swirled around us off a beautiful reef in a place called the Gardens of the Queen.*

of basking shark fins have sold for more than $10,000. Unless shark finning is stopped, many species will become extinct.

Sharks around the world are in big trouble, and time is running out. Some species are almost 90 percent gone. Sharks take many years to reproduce, and now more sharks are killed each year than are born.

But there is some good news. A few shark populations are protected and growing. Some countries have created protected areas and no-fishing zones.

Shark tourism is popular. People pay to cage dive with great white sharks, to snorkel with whale sharks, and to watch professional shark feeds. Some people say shark tourism is a bad idea because it may make sharks less afraid of humans. But others think that if people appreciate sharks, they'll help protect them. Sharks help keep nature in balance. A sea without sharks would be an empty sea.

HOW YOU CAN HELP

One way to help sharks is to become an expert on them. You are already on your way! Learn as much about sharks as you can. Read about sharks in books and on the Internet. Tell friends and relatives what you've learned. They will be surprised that there are so many species, that sharks take a long time to have pups, and that many could go extinct.

■ Do a science project on sharks and share what you have learned with your classmates. Send an e-mail to an aquarium or zoo for information. Some aquariums have live webcasts, so you can watch sharks on your computer and submit questions.

◀ *Sharks in movies and at amusement parks—such as this mechanical shark at Universal Studios in California—are often shown as fearsome predators who want to eat people. The truth is, sharks are at much greater risk from humans than we are from sharks.*

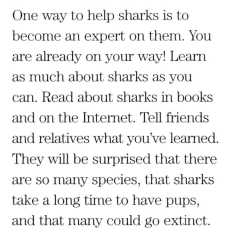

■ Don't buy shark jaws and shark food products. Go to the fish counter at the supermarket or a fish market and see if sharks are being sold. Try to learn what sharks they are. If the sharks are from species whose populations are declining, ask your parents to help you write a letter to the store owner. Tell them you are concerned about sharks. If you see shark fin soup on a menu, write a letter to the restaurant. Ask them to stop serving this dish.

■ Many wildlife conservation organizations are involved in saving sharks. For example, the World Wildlife Fund, Wild Aid, Oceana, and the Shark Research Institute have up-to-date information on shark conservation. Go to their Web sites to learn more about ways you can help.

■ Imagine having a fund-raiser for sharks! Find a conservation organization with a shark project you would like to support. Think about ways to raise money. With all that you've learned about sharks, you could be a big help!

IT'S YOUR TURN

■ Spend time with sharks. Visit an aquarium and watch sharks. Take a notebook and make some sketches. Take notes about how they move and how they interact with other fish. Many sharks, like nurse sharks and sand tiger sharks, do well in aquariums. Some aquariums have special shark programs. The Georgia Aquarium in Atlanta has

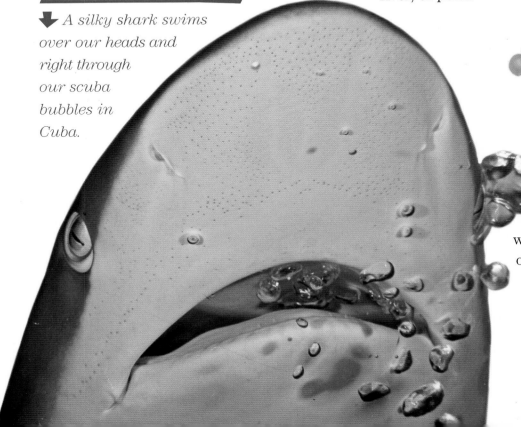

▼ *A silky shark swims over our heads and right through our scuba bubbles in Cuba.*

whale sharks that were rescued from fishermen. The Monterey Bay Aquarium in California has a catch-and-release program for juvenile great white sharks.

■ Do you ever look out over a body of water and wonder what lives there and how it lives and where it goes? We wonder about that all the time. Do you ever think about swimming underwater and taking pictures of sharks and rays and other fish? You can start by getting comfortable in water. Any water will do: a pool, lake, river, or pond.

Learn to wear a mask, fins, and a snorkel. Learn to watch things underwater. Always ask your parents before you go swimming and make sure there is an adult watching you. We never work underwater or dive alone. We always have a water buddy.

■ Think like a shark. They can "feel" their prey's faint electrical field from a distance. In the water, try to locate your friends with your eyes closed. Look up through the water toward the surface. Do the people look a little like seals?

■ Which sea creatures would you like to photograph? Learn where they live and how you could get to them. What interests you about these animals? Would you like to know more about the foods they eat? The ways they move? The regions of the ocean they live in?

FACTS AT A GLANCE

Ichthyologist and shark expert Dr. Eugenie Clark examines two sets of great white shark jaws in the fish collection of the British Museum of London, England.

Scientific Name

Sharks belong to the class Chondrichthyes, along with skates and rays. These fish have skeletons made of cartilage.

Common Names

Sharks are often referred to by their common names, but some have many names. Sand tiger sharks are also called ragged tooth sharks (or raggies). Great white sharks are called white sharks and white pointers. Horn sharks are also called pig sharks and Port Jackson sharks.

Size

Whale sharks are the biggest, up to 40 feet (12 meters) long and up to 15.5 tons (14 m tons) in weight. The six-inch lantern sharks are the smallest.

Life Span

No one really knows how long a shark can live. Some species of sharks live 15 to 20 years, and others may live up to 100.

Special Features

Sharks are so well adapted to their environments that their basic body type has remained unchanged for millions of years. Their streamlined body shapes make them fast, efficient swimmers. Their amazing senses of smell, hearing, touch, and electroreception help them hone in on prey. They break down their food slowly, so they can go as long as two months without food if needed. Some warm-bodied sharks keep their body temperatures up to 10° F warmer than the surrounding water. This ability keeps their muscles warm, so they can swim faster and be better hunters.

Habitat

Sharks live everywhere in the sea, from ankle-deep water down to a mile or more below the surface. They patrol the open ocean (or pelagic zone) and near the seashore, from the hot tropics to cool temperate waters and Arctic seas. Bull sharks swim far upstream into freshwater lakes and rivers.

Food

Almost all sharks are meat eaters, or carnivores. They

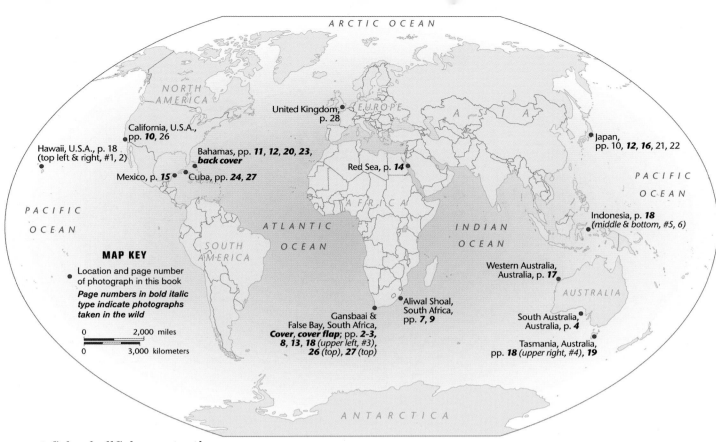

MAP KEY

• Location and page number
  of photograph in this book

*Page numbers in bold italic
type indicate photographs
taken in the wild*

0 ————— 2,000 miles

0 ————— 3,000 kilometers

United Kingdom, p. 28

California, U.S.A., pp. *10*, 26

Hawaii, U.S.A., p. 18
(top left & right, #1, 2)

Bahamas, pp. *11*, *12*, *20*, *23*,
back cover

Mexico, p. *15*   Cuba, pp. *24*, *27*

Red Sea, p. 14

Japan,
pp. 10, *12*, *16*, 21, 22

Indonesia, p. *18*
(middle & bottom, #5, 6)

Western Australia,
Australia, p. *17*

Aliwal Shoal,
South Africa,
pp. *7*, *9*

South Australia,
Australia, p. 4

Gansbaai &
False Bay, South Africa,
Cover, cover flap; pp. *2-3*,
8, *13*, *18* (upper left, #3),
26 (top), *27* (top)

Tasmania, Australia,
pp. *18* (upper right, #4), *19*

ARCTIC OCEAN

NORTH AMERICA

EUROPE

ASIA

PACIFIC OCEAN

PACIFIC OCEAN

ATLANTIC OCEAN

AFRICA

INDIAN OCEAN

SOUTH AMERICA

AUSTRALIA

ANTARCTICA

eat fish, shellfish, sea turtles, marine mammals, and some sea birds. Some, like the whale shark, are filter feeders and eat plankton. Others, such as tiger sharks, are famous for eating just about anything they find, even a car's license plates. They have been found with chicken coops, bags of potatoes, pajamas, shoes, rubber tires, and cans of Spam in their stomachs.

▬ Reproduction

Baby sharks grow slowly inside their mother's body. It can take from 18 to 22 months before they are born. A mother shark can have from 2 to 135 pups. The babies know how to swim and hunt as soon as they're born, and they typically leave their mothers right away. Most sharks give birth to live babies, but a few species of sharks lay eggs.

▬ Biggest Threats

Humans are the biggest threat to sharks. Sharks are caught for food and sport, and others

↑ Sharks are found in all the oceans of the world.

are killed by accident on longlines and in nets set for other fish. Having too many houses and buildings on coasts causes water pollution, which hurts sharks. Although shark attacks are the subject of many scary books and movies, only about six people a year are actually killed by sharks—compared with 100 million sharks killed by people.

GLOSSARY

Bycatch: Sharks (or other animals) that are caught by accident in nets or on fishing lines intended to catch other species. The bycatch is usually thrown away.

Cartilage: The stiff substance that shark skeletons are made of. Your nose and ears are made of cartilage too.

Dermal denticles: Tiny, tooth-like scales on a shark's skin.

Dorsal fin: The fin on the back of a shark, whale, or dolphin. It helps keep the animal upright in the water and helps it make fast turns.

Electroreception: The ability to sense the electrical field around living creatures.

Finning: Cutting off a shark's fin and dumping the animal back in the water to die.

Longline: A long fishing line with hundreds or thousands of hooks that commercial fishermen use. Some longlines are set to catch sharks, and some are set to catch other fish.

Pelagic zone: The open ocean.

Plankton: Microscopic organisms that live in the ocean. Filter feeders, such as whale sharks, swim through the ocean and strain out the plankton to eat.

Predator: An animal that preys on other animals as food.

Rostrum: A long snout that is edged with teeth. Sharks that have rostrums use them to find food and to attack prey.

FIND OUT MORE

Books & Articles
Clarke, Penny, and Mark Bergin. *Sharks.* East Sussex, England: Book House, 2002.

Claybourne, Anna. *1000 Facts on Sharks.* Essex, England: Miles Kelly Publishing, 2004.

Llewellyn, Claire, et al. *The Best Book of Sharks.* London, England: Kingfisher, 1999.

Simon, Seymour. *Sharks.* New York: HarperCollins Publishers, 1995.

Films
Sharkwater (2006). (PG) A documentary with amazing footage of sharks that covers shark biology and exposes the cruelty of shark finning. http://www.imdb.com/title/tt0856008

Web Sites
Learn all about sharks, get tips for avoiding shark attacks, and play shark word games at the Florida Museum of Natural History's Web site at http://www.flmnh.ufl.edu/fish/Kids/kids.htm.

You can watch videos of sharks hunting at http://dsc.discovery.com/sharks/shark-videos.

See sharks swimming live on the Waikiki Aquarium's Shark Cam in Hawaii at http://www.waquarium.org/sharkcam/index.html, or on the Minnesota Zoo Shark Cam at http://www.channel4000.com/sharkcam/index.html.

Check out the National Geographic pages: http://kids.nationalgeographic.com/Animals/CreatureFeature/Great-white-shark.

INDEX

Boldface *indicates illustrations.*

Aquariums 27

Babies *see* Pups
Body temperature 28
Breach behavior **8**
Breathing 15, 23
Bycatch 22, 30

Cartilage 9, 28, 30
Catch-and-release program 27
Claspers 13
Common names 28
Conservation 21–26
Coral reefs 21, 25

Dermal denticles 13, 30
Dorsal fins 30

Eggs **10,** 13, 29
Electroreception 6, 910, 27, 28, 30
Eyesight 10–11

Facts at a glance 28
Filter feeders 16, 19, 29, 30
Finning 22–23, 25, 30
Fins **21,** 22–23, 25, 30
Fishermen 5, 21–22, 27, 30
Food 11, 12, 16, 19, 28–29, 30

Glossary 30

Habitat 15, 28
Hearing, sense of 28
How you can help 26

Ichthyologists 16

Jaws 26, **28**

Lifespan 28
Longlines 15, 21, 29, 30

Map 29
Metabolism 28, 30

Nictitating membrane 11
No-fishing zones 25

Pelagic zone 28, 30
Photographing sharks 5, 6, 27, 81
Plankton 18, 19, 29, 30
Pups
    birth of 6, **11,** 13, 29
    litter sizes 13, 22, 29
    survival of 5, 13
    unborn pups 5, 22, 29

Reproduction 12–13, 29
    birth of pups 6, **11,** 13, 29
    egg laying 10, 13, 29
    low rate of 25, 26, 29
    pregnancy 13, 29
Rostrums 6, 19, 30

Scientific name 28
Shark attacks 6, 19, 29, 30
Shark cages **4,** 5, 6, 7, 25, 31
Shark-fin soup 21, 22, 26
Shark fishing 5, 21–22
Shark liver oil 22
Shark tourism 25
Sizes and shapes 15, 16, 18, 28
Skeletons 9, 28, 30
Skin 13, 30
Smell, sense of 9, 28
Species, number of 16, 18
Swimming safety tips 6, 27
Swimsuits
    designed like shark skin 13

Teeth **9,** 11–12, **12,** 19, 30
Threats, biggest 29
Touch, sense of 28

RESEARCH & PHOTOGRAPHIC NOTES

The hardest part of making good shark pictures is finding sharks. We used to see sharks on almost every dive. Now we can work underwater for a long time and never see a shark because so many have been caught and killed.

Our job is not easy, but it is always an adventure. To make a picture underwater, we put our Nikon cameras into a special waterproof container called an underwater housing. The housing has a glass port or bubble in front of the camera lens called a dome that allows us to see. We use electronic flashes, or strobes, on the end of long arms attached to the camera housing to light up the sharks. The camera and long arms look a lot like a giant spider or crab.

You must get close to a shark to get a good picture, and you have to take many pictures to get just a few good ones. We go to sea with scientists and expert guides who know shark behavior and can help us get close and stay safe. The scientists teach us about sharks and help us see different behavior that we would not see on our own.

We have different ways to photograph different sharks. For the whale and basking sharks, we wear mask, fins, and snorkel and swim as fast as we can with our cameras to keep up with them. When we work with guides who feed sharks, we always pay attention to the rules and cover all of our skin and wear gloves. (our skin looks like bait to a hungry shark.) To photograph great white sharks, we work with experts who put a smelly oil chum slick into the water to let the sharks know where we are. With white sharks, we always work inside a metal cage to protect us.

The most important thing is to be watchful, aware, and careful. In large groups of sharks, we always photograph back to back so we are watching in all directions. Even though many sharks are gentle and calm, we respect all sharks as wild predators and never touch them. When they appear agitated or out of control, we always leave the water.

We have shared great moments with these wonderful creatures, and we hope that good pictures of sharks will make people want to learn more about them and want to protect them.   —DD & JH

FOR DR. EUGENIE CLARK, THE
SHARK LADY. SHE OPENED THE
DOOR TO THE WORLD OF SHARKS.
—DD & JH

Acknowledgments
Every successful story has a successful
team behind it. Scientists, guides, natu-
ralists, boat captains, and assistants are
the backbone to every picture. Making
shark images is not easy, but we have
had the good fortune of working with
very knowledgeable "sharky" people
around the world who work hard to
know more about sharks and work even
harder to keep them swimming on this
planet. We would like to extend our fins
in a hearty thank you to Rodney Fox and
Karen Gowlett-Holmes of Australia and
Andre Hartman, Mark and Gail Addison,
and Chris Fallows and Charles Maxwell
of South Africa. We also wish to thank
Yves LeFevre, Koji Nakamura, Jim Watt,
Stuart Cove, and the invincible scientists
Dr. Gerry Allan, Dr. Eugenie Clark, Dr.
Sonny Gruber, and Dr. Jack Randall.
—David Doubilet and Jennifer Hayes

Book design by David M. Seager.
The body text of the book is set in
ITC Century. The display text is set
in Knockout and Party Noid.

Front cover: A great white shark off
Gansbaai, South Africa, flashes rows of
teeth sharper than daggers. *Cover flap:*
Tiger sharks like this one are famous
for eating just about anything. *Back
cover:* David Doubilet on assignment
with Caribbean reef sharks off
Nassau, Bahamas.

Published by the
National Geographic Society

John M. Fahey, Jr., *President and
Chief Executive Officer*

Gilbert M. Grosvenor,
Chairman of the Board

Tim T. Kelly,
President, Global Media Group

John Q. Griffin,
President, Publishing

Nina D. Hoffman, *Executive Vice
President; President, Book
Publishing Group*

Staff for This Book

Nancy Laties Feresten, *Vice President,
Editor-in-Chief of Children's Books*

Bea Jackson, *Design and Illustrations
Director, Children's Books*

Amy Shields, *Executive Editor*

Jennifer Emmett, Mary Beth Oelkers-
Keegan, *Project Editors*

David M. Seager, *Art Director*

Lori Epstein, *Illustrations Editor*

Jocelyn G. Lindsay, *Researcher*

Carl Mehler, *Director of Maps*

Felita Vereen-Mills, *Senior
Administrative Assistant*

Jennifer Thornton, *Managing Editor*

Grace Hill, *Associate Managing Editor*

R. Gary Colbert, *Production Director*

Lewis R. Bassford, *Production Manager*

Rachel Faulise, Nicole Elliott,
Manufacturing Managers

Susan Borke, *Legal and Business
Affairs*

The publisher gratefully acknowledges
the assistance of Christine Kiel, K-3
curriculum and reading consultant.

Library of Congress
Cataloging-in-Publication Data

Doubilet, David.
 Face to face with sharks / by David Doubilet
and Jennifer Hayes.
    p. cm.
 Includes bibliographical references and
index.
 ISBN 978-1-4263-0404-0 (hardcover : alk.
paper)—ISBN 978-1-4263-0405-7 (library
binding : alk. paper)
1. Sharks—Juvenile literature. 2. Sharks—
Pictorial works. I. Hayes, Jennifer. II. Title.
QL638.9.D68 2009
597.3--dc22

2008038244

Founded in 1888, the National Geographic
Society is one of the largest nonprofit scientific and educational organizations in the
world. It reaches more than 285 million
people worldwide each month through its
official journal, NATIONAL GEOGRAPHIC, and
its four other magazines; the National
Geographic Channel; television documen-
taries; radio programs; films; books; videos
and DVDs; maps; and interactive media.
National Geographic has funded more than
8,000 scientific research projects and
supports an education program combating
geographic illiteracy.

For more information, please call
1-800-NGS LINE (647-5463)
or write to the following address:

National Geographic Society
1145 17th Street N.W.
Washington, D.C. 20036-4688 U.S.A.

Visit us online at
www.nationalgeographic.com/books.
Librarians and teachers, visit us at
www.ngchildrensbooks.com. Kids and parents,
visit us at kids.nationalgeographic.com.

For information about special discounts
for bulk purchases, please contact
National Geographic Books Special Sales:
ngspecsales@ngs.org. For rights or permis-
sions inquiries, please contact National
Geographic Books Subsidiary Rights:
ngbookrights@ngs.org.

Printed in China

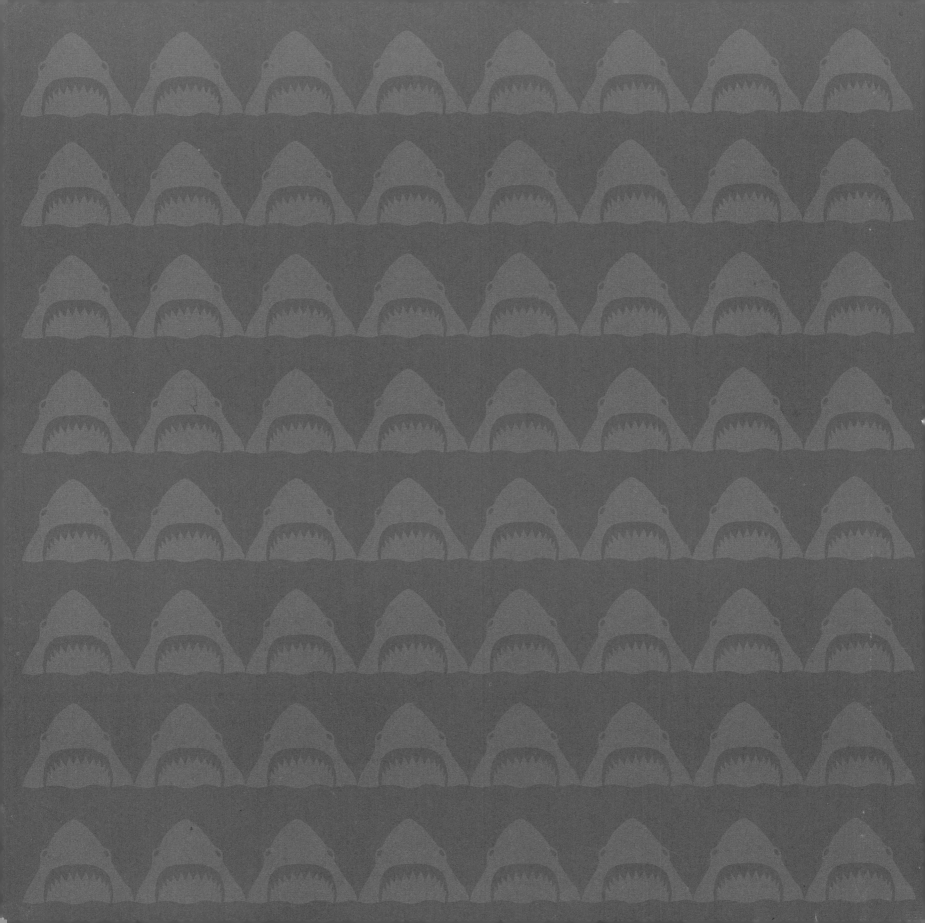